PARABLES OF GOLF

PARABLES

of

GOLF

Gathered by

EDMOND G. EBERTS

ↄ൦ *References revered* ↄ൦

Boarish Press
Montreal, Canada

BOARISH PRESS
426 Lansdowne Avenue
Westmount, Quebec
Canada H3Y 2V2

Canadian Cataloguing in Publication Data

Eberts, Edmond G. (Edmond Gordon), 1938–
    Parables of golf

    Includes bibliographical references.
    ISBN 0-9698807-0-7

    1. Golf. 2. Golf – History. 3. Golf courses – Design and construction –
    History. 4. Golf in art. I. Title.

GV963.E24 1995   796.352   C95-900977-9

Legal deposit, Bibliothèque nationale du Québec, fourth quarter 1995

Designed and typeset by J.M. Eberts
Photography by See Spot Run Inc.
Author portrait by Sherman Hines

Printed and bound in Canada on acid free paper by
Imprimerie Gagné ltée, Louiseville, Quebec

For further information:
telephone: (800) 363-8134 or (416) 366-9264
fax: (416) 366-1855
or write to:
The Turnberry Tour, Suite 703, 141 Adelaide Street West
Toronto, Ontario, Canada M5H 3L5

DEDICATION

Parables of Golf is dedicated to all those who respect the traditions of the game and foster its development worldwide. The raison d'être is to raise funds in support of junior golf and caddie programmes.

Thirty percent of golf club and proshop sales will go directly to the respective club programmes, the balance and net bookstore proceeds will be contributed towards scholarships granted by the likes of the Canadian Golf Foundation, the Evans Scholars Foundation, the Francis Ouimet Scholarship Fund and the Robert T. Jones, Jr. Foundation in the United States, The Golf Foundation in Britain, the New Zealand Golf Association and the Australian Golf Union, wherever the book is sold.

CONTENTS

PREFACE

The four parables you are about to peruse were inspired by a variety of books and periodicals, and gathered together at intervals between 1989 and 1994. They reflect what I and many other golfing partisans consider to be the intrinsic aspects of the game.

More recently I had the good fortune to acquire *Thanks for the Game, the best of golf with Henry Cotton,* first published in 1980 in Great Britain by Sidgwick and Jackson Limited. The Maestro (1907–1987) was a three-time winner who celebrated his fiftieth appearance in the Open Championship at Turnberry, Scotland, in 1977, the very year that Tom Watson defeated Jack Nicklaus on the final hole in what some are calling the finest golf match ever.

Starting in 1960, one of Henry Cotton's greatest and most rewarding pleasures was to select and award the rookie of the year in Britain. Tony Jacklin, Bernard Gallagher and Sandy Lyle are but three honourees who have subsequently earned worldwide recognition. To his star rookies he expounded four *Rules of Life* for any champion. Every young golfer and caddie would be wise to heed his advice.

With the kind permission of his publisher, may Henry Cotton's words of wisdom serve as an appropriate preface for *Parables of Golf.*

1. Live for something other than yourself. If you only think of yourself you will find thousands of reasons for being unhappy; you will never have had the treatment which you thought you deserved, and you will never have done all you wanted to do or should have done. Build up a present of which you can be proud. Whoever lives for a purpose – for his country, for others less fortunate, for his family – forgets his own troubles and worries.

2. Act, instead of lamenting the absurdities of this world. We must try to transform our own small lot. We can't hope to change the universe, but then our objectives are smaller. To do your own job well and become a master at it is not always easy, but you will find happiness in working hard and making a success of your job, whatever it might be.

3. You must believe in the power of your own will. I do not believe that the future is completely predetermined. Whoever has the courage and strength of will can, to a certain extent, control his destiny. Obviously, we are not all-powerful. Individual freedom has its limits, but freedom lies between the boundaries of things that are possible and our own will. We must always discipline ourselves without thinking of the limitations. Laziness and cowardice are weaknesses, work and courage are acts of will. And strength of purpose is, perhaps, the queen of virtues.

4. Never deceive. Faithfulness is perhaps as valuable as strength of purpose. It is not an easy virtue. You must be true to your promises, to your contracts, to others and to yourself.

These rules are very harsh but you must add to them a sense of humour – it will enable you to smile at yourself, and with others.

Thank you Mr. Henry Cotton.

ACKNOWLEDGEMENTS

At the outset I'd like to acknowledge my great-uncle Bob, Robert E. MacDougall, who introduced me to the game of golf, providing several sets of hickory-shafted clubs, hundreds of brand-new, tissue-wrapped Silver King golf balls and early morning lessons at the Tadoussac Golf Club. The professionals who have subsequently instructed me include: Andy Black, Lenny Harmon, Pat Fletcher, Norm Hunt, Don Price and Phil Hardy. The third-mentioned was the last native-born winner of the Canadian Open back in 1954!

While I had the good fortune to master the art of fly-fishing thanks to my dear father, it was my wonderful mother who encouraged me to pursue my passion for golf. I would also like to thank my wife, Maureen, and my daughters, Jennifer, Rachael and Katie, who have fortuitously come to appreciate my love of the game, its traditions and intrigue. My brother Jay was kind enough to sort out my writings and publish *Parables of Golf* for all to enjoy.

Finally, I should mention and thank Robert Macdonald, publisher of The Classics of Golf, and his eminent collaborator, Herbert Warren Wind, for providing an ever-growing library of remarkable books to read and to cherish, and for allowing me to use copyrighted material, rather than subjecting readers to a second-best paraphrasing.

1

THE ROYAL AND ANCIENT GAME OF GOLF

Introduction

Robert Clark's *Golf, a Royal and Ancient Game*, first published in 1875, includes extracts from an immense variety of documents bearing on the history of the game. Notwithstanding, the best collation of the most important golfing developments with the historical events that gave rise to them is found in Robert Browning's masterpiece, *A History of Golf*, first published in 1955.

The purpose of this dissertation is to share glimpses of Robert Browning's insight into the history of the royal and ancient game of golf and Charles Blair Macdonald's commentary on course design as mentioned in his classic *Scotland's Gift – Golf*.

Ancient History

Despite all other historic speculation, the fact remains that it was the Scots who devised the essential features of golf, the combination of hitting for distance with the final nicety of an approach to an exiguous mark, and the independent progress of each player with his own ball, free from interference by his adversary. Golf was a widely popular game by 1457.

It is also possible that the word *golf* originally referred to the club not the game, the word *tee* to the place from which the player was entitled to *strike off*. The word *green* meant the whole course and still survives in this sense in the phrases *green committee*, *greenkeeper* and *through the green*. Even today the English Golf Union uses the word in its old sense in official announcements, for example, *next year's championship will be played on the green of such and such a club*.

In early golf the words *drive* or *driver* were not used. Rather the golfer *struck off* from the tee with a *play-club;* and he did not *drive* towards a selected landmark, he *played upon it*. The word *fore* likely derives from the military expression *ware before* – look out in front – the signal for the defenders of the gate to drop to the ground in order that the guns might be fired over them; not dissimilar to a golfer intending to hit over the head of someone on the fairway in front. Even today, fore is the most democratic of shouts which no one dares to let pass unheeded!

The term *links* gives rise to a certain amount of controversy as there is a modern-day tendency to restrict the term to the natural seaside golf country among the sand dunes and applied only to courses of this traditional type. However, links historically and more correctly refers to an expanse of turf in Scotland, the English equivalent being *downs*.

More unfortunate is the divergence in the use of the term *bogey*. In British golf the bogey of a hole was the par figure, the score which a first-class golfer might be expected to take. But as playing standards improved, bogey figures were not tightened up sufficiently rapidly. As a result there was a tendency for the bogey scores to be one stroke more than par at three or four holes out of the eighteen, on the majority of courses. Unluckily this seems to have given American golfers the idea that bogey is one over par at every hole and on the western side of the Atlantic has become a term of contempt!

Modern History

The modern history of golf begins with the formation of the first golf clubs in the middle of the eighteenth century. The courses were wholly natural; the only greenkeepers were the rabbits. Competitions – apart from private matches – were unknown. Nobody had thought of keeping score! Rules were simple and few, and framed to meet local conditions. All distinctions of rank were levelled by the joyous spirit of the game.

Notwithstanding, even in these Arcadian days, the prowess of the leading players would be a matter of popular discussion in their own towns.

Political clubs were likely the first. It was only by a slow and gradual process that the club idea was extended to apply to sport. In the case of golf the creation of the clubs was the indirect and unforeseen result of the first attempt to run an open meeting.

In 1744 several gentlemen of honour petitioned the City of Edinburgh to provide a silver club for annual competition on the links of Leith and the magistrates agreed to provide the trophy. The winner was to be called the *captain of the golf* – or as we would nowadays say, the champion golfer – and was to be the arbitrator of all disputes touching the game.

However, there were few outside competitors from other clubs and in 1764 the Leith captains of golf – the previous winners of the competition – successfully petitioned the City of Edinburgh for authority *to admit such Noblemen and Gentlemen as they approve to be Members of the Company of Golfers,* and to restrict the competition for the silver club to these members. Thereby the contest for the trophy became a club competition.

In sum, the formation of almost every golf club was the presentation of a trophy for competition, and the first competition for the silver club on the 7th of March 1744 is assumed to be the beginning of the Honourable Company of Edinburgh Golfers. The second group to subscribe for a silver club was the Society of St. Andrews Golfers, and the inaugural competition was held on the 14th of May 1754. Subsequently, in 1834, King William IV issued the charter forming the Royal and Ancient Golf Club of St. Andrews (R&A).

The founding of the Montreal Golf Club in 1873 marked the organization of the very first golf club in North America, bestowed the *Royal* title by Queen Victoria in 1884. The first permanent club in the United States, the St. Andrew's Golf Club in Yonkers, New York, was founded four years later in 1877.

One of the results of the development of the convivial side of golf club activities was the gradual abandonment of the practice of deciding the captaincy by the result of annual competition. However, at St. Andrews there remains a curious system by which the choice of captain is determined by the past-captains sitting in solemn conclave, other clubs deciding by a combination of election and competition.

Why Eighteen Holes Make a Round

During the half century which succeeded the formation of the first golf clubs, the Honourable Company of Edinburgh Golfers set the mode for the rest and took an unquestioned lead in framing the rules of the game. That the Honourable Company failed to retain this proud position must be attributed to the gradual deterioration of the Leith links, which faded out of popularity as the fame of St. Andrews grew early in the nineteenth century to become recognized as the golfing capital of the world.

The earliest documentary evidence of the playing of golf at St. Andrews takes the form of a licence dated 25th January 1552 confirming *the rycht and possessioun, propirtie and communite of the saidis liniks.* It will be noted that this is not an original grant, merely a confirmation of rights already established by long usage.

One of the first and most important results of the substitution of St. Andrews for Leith as the capital of golf was the adoption of eighteen holes as the recognized round. In the first half of the nineteenth century the figure varied from the five of the original Leith layout to the twenty-five of Montrose.

At St. Andrews golfers played eleven holes out to the far end of the course, then turned and played eleven holes home, playing to the same holes as on the outward journey but in reverse direction. In 1764, however, the R&A passed a resolution that the four first holes should be converted into two and, as this change automatically converted the same four holes into two on the road in, the *round* was thereby reduced from twenty-two to eighteen.

It was not long afterwards that the St. Andrews golfers discovered the advisability of having separate fairways and holes for the outward and homeward journeys. It is to this peculiar arrangement of the Old Course that we owe the familiar phrases *out* and *home.*

The Evolution of the Caddie

One of the few golfing terms whose derivation appears to admit of no dispute is the title given the henchman who carries clubs. The word *caddie* is merely the Scottish spelling of the French word *cadet.*

Later on the designation was applied by Scottish sarcasm to the hangers-on who, in the eighteenth century, loafed about the streets of Edinburgh, ready to run errands or do any sort of odd jobs; and so caddie came to mean a porter, long before its application began to be restricted to the particular kind of porter who carries a golfer's clubs.

The first caddie whose name has come down to us was one Andrew Dickson, who caddied for the Duke of York, afterwards James II, in 1681 and 1682 at the links at Leith. The caddie's fee was equivalent to fourpence.

To the purist of golfing speech there is no verb *to caddie.* The word carry, however, is used in the same purely technical sense, as is shown by the famous retort of the caddie whose employer had left a jacket in the clubhouse and wanted his caddie to go back for it: *Go back for it yersel! I'm paid to carry, no' to fetch and carry!*

The caddie is recognized by the rules of the game as part of the *side.* He is the only person from whom the side may ask advice as to the club to take, or the shot to play, and on the other hand his sins of omission or commission – accidently interfering with an opponent's ball, or the like – involve the same penalties as if they had been committed by the player himself.

The modern golfer may describe his caddie *as something between a hindrance and a help* and complain that he seems to know everything about golf and nothing whatever about caddying, but in the old days he was his patron's guide, philosopher and friend, his instructor when he was off his game, and co-arbiter with the opposition caddie in all disputes.

It is late in the history of the game before we catch a glimpse of the caddie as a player. The date of the transition from the status of senior caddie to professional is fairly clearly defined. David Robertson was the last of the senior caddies, his son Allan the first of the great professionals, circa 1823. Allan enjoyed the distinction of being the first player to ever break eighty for St. Andrews links, doing a seventy-nine in 1858!

Start of the Championships

The golden age of private matches was brought to an end by the inauguration of the first championships in the middle of the nineteenth century. The whole credit for this development belongs to the Prestwick Club, and the history of championship golf really begins with a letter sent out to seven other leading clubs on the 6th of April 1857. The response was immediate and enthusiastic with thirteen entries in all! The wishes of the majority fixed on St. Andrews as the scene of the tournament, and it was duly carried out on the last three days of July.

A year later, with twenty-eight entries, the idea of club foursomes was abandoned in favour of an individual contest. The winner was Robert Chambers.

In 1860, the Prestwick Club, with the amateur championship apparently well established at St. Andrews, turned its thoughts to a similar event for professionals. A challenge belt of red morocco, richly ornamented with massive silver plates, and costing the handsome sum of thirty guineas, was substituted for the originally proposed medal.

Eight players entered the event, decided over three rounds of the twelve-hole Prestwick links. This first contest for the challenge belt is spoken of as the first Open Championship, all too often misnamed the British Open. The first meeting was open to professionals only and this restriction was removed a year later. Old Tom Morris and the elder Willie Park respectively won four and three of the first eight championships!

The first English professional to beat the Scots at their own game and win the Open Championship, which he held four times subsequent to his 1894 victory, was John Henry Taylor of Westward Ho!, the Royal North Devon Club, founded in 1864.

From Feathery to Rubber Core

It is generally assumed that the earliest golf balls were the leather balls stuffed with feathers which were still in use up to the middle of the nineteenth century, but it is much more probable that in the early days of golf the balls were turned boxwood.

Feathery ball-making was a fine art. The leather cover was stitched first, leaving only a small hole open. Through this hole the soaked feathers were thrust in by means of an iron spike fixed in a wooden framework upon which the ball maker leant all his weight for the better compression of the stuffing. After drying, the feathers expanded and the leather contracted, resulting in an extremely hard mass which was hammered into roundness and painted white.

With regard to distance to which the feathery balls could be driven, the Glasgow Club records of 1786 mention a player named John Gibson making a series of drives ranging in distance from 182 to 222 yards. At first, featheries flew further than the *gutties* but they were seldom perfectly spherical, were apt to become waterlogged in wet weather, were ruined as soon as one hack with an iron club broke the surface of the distended leather, and cost what seemed the extravagant sum of half a crown apiece. Gutties were, by contrast, practically indestructible.

A poem by William Graham, written for a meeting of the Innerleven Club, fixes the date of the coming into use of the *gutta-percha* balls at 1848. Though they did not at once drive the older balls out of the field, the loss of revenue from ball-making was far more than made up for by the vast increase in the number of players taking up the game.

Even so, the guttie made the game distinctly hard work, for the player had to do the whole work of getting it up in the air; and its unyielding solidity frequently gave an unpleasant jar to the player's arm if he mishit a shot with an iron club.

Notwithstanding, golfers soon discovered that a ball's flight was significantly longer and more accurate after it had been nicked through use. The hard-hammered gutta ball (1870–80) was followed by iron moulds and presses for creating consistent, detailed surface textures and patterns, circa 1890.

All this was changed by the advent of the rubber-cored ball at the beginning of the present century. The new balls were the invention of a Cleveland, Ohio, golfer named Coburn Haskell and were brought into production by the Goodrich Rubber Company.

The first *Haskell* ball did not outdrive the gutta ball by any exaggerated extent; that was to come later. It is perhaps a pity that it was not allowed to remain so, for as time went on the ingenuity of manufacturers reduced the thickness of the cover, increased the tension of the winding, substituted a liquid centre for the solid core, and by reducing the size and increasing the weight, produced a missile capable of being propelled over ever-increasing distances with the trajectory of a bullet. *The only result was to give golfers more and more walking for fewer shots!*

The Development of Golf Architecture

The coming of the guttie ball, which reduced the expense of the game by two-thirds, brought an immense influx of new players onto the course. At the same time, the use of iron clubs through the green gradually cut down the gorse and vents along either edge of the fairway, which in consequence became appreciably widened.

Mending of the turf probably involved no more than the repair of divot marks in the immediate vicinity of the hole, which was still the teeing ground as well as the putting green. Nobody had yet conceived the fantastic notion that the putting greens should be mown and rolled!

The golf boom led to construction of innumerable courses in private parks. However, they tended to make the course a steeplechase rather than a point-to-point affair. Finally, come the turn of this century, golf architecture became one of the fine arts and, except as regards the difficulties arising from a sea breeze, the best inland courses became as stiff a test of the game as the most famous of the older seaside links.

Charles Blair Macdonald (1872–1927), a founding member of the USGA in 1894 and winner of the inaugural US Amateur Championship a year later, was the first great American golf-course architect. In *Scotland's Gift – Golf* he reminisces:

Diversity in nature is universal. Let your golfing architect mirror it. An ideal or classical golf course demands variety, personality and, above all, the charm of romance. Don't sacrifice accuracy for length!

A golf hole, humanly speaking, is like life, inasmuch as one cannot judge justly of any person's character the first time one meets him. Sometimes it takes years to discover and appreciate hidden qualities which only time discloses, and he usually discloses them on the links. No real lover of golf with artistic understanding would undertake to measure the quality or fascination of a golf hole by a yardstick, any more than a critic of poetry would attempt to measure the supreme sentiment expressed in a poem by the same method. One can understand the meter, but one cannot measure the soul expressed. It is absolutely inconceivable.

Modern golf, though perhaps a stiffer test of a player's skill, has robbed the game of some of its charm as an adventure of the spirit!

Wind I consider the finest asset (invisible hazard) in golf: in itself it is one of the greatest and most delightful accompaniments in the game. Without wind your course is always the same, but as the wind varies in velocity and from various points of the compass, you not only have one course but you have many courses. Experts of the game temper their shots to the wind and learn how to make the most of it, pulling or slicing it at will into the wind or hitting a low ball into the face of the wind. It is here that a true golfer excels.

Therefore, in designing a course try to lay out the holes so as they vary in direction. That way a player gets an opportunity to play all the varying wind shots in a round.

Evolution of the Rules

Prior to the inauguration of the first competitions at Leith and St. Andrews, there was no need for any established code of rules. The original *Articles and Laws in playing the Golf* date back to 1744 and were admirably brief!

One of the chief difficulties in the establishment of a universal code of rules was that while the St. Andrews' code was designed for match play, with an addendum of modifications for stroke competitions, the rest of the world regarded stroke play as the basis of the game and would have preferred a code of rules primarily designed for that. A universal code was only achieved as the result of a joint revision of the rules by the Royal and Ancient Golf Club and the United States Golf Association at a conference in 1951!

The chief feature of the new code was the final establishment of loss of stroke and distance as the penalty for ball out of bounds, unplayable ball, and lost ball. In addition, a *no stymies* rule was formally adopted.

Unfortunately many an *unsophisticated* golfer has come to feel *entitled* to a fair smack at the ball thus the excuse for the application of *winter rules* to allow for the ball being teed up through the green. From a greenkeeping point of view, however, such a rule tends to defeat its own objective, since it leads to the best spots of turf being destroyed! Thus winter rules for the avoidance of bad lies should not be encouraged and no score under winter rules can be accepted as a *record* of any kind!

Methods of Scoring

In the early days of golf the only form of play was a match between two opposing sides, decided by holes. In a St. Andrews' minute dated 9th May 1759, *it is enacted and agreed by the captain and the gentlemen golfers present that, in all time coming, whoever puts in the ball at the fewest strokes over the field shall be declared and sustained victor.* Thus stroke play had finally been invented.

Afterword

I hope that my abridgement of Robert Browning's *A History of Golf* and Charles Blair Macdonald's commentary on golf-course design will encourage all who would be golfers to learn more about the traditions of this magnificent game.

If I may, I would like to leave you with an afterword, as attributed to Arthur James, the first Earl of Balfour (1848–1930), often referred to as the father of English golf: *Give me my books, my golf clubs, and leisure, and I would ask for nothing more. My ideal life is to read a lot, write a little, play plenty of golf, and have nothing to worry about!* Enjoy.

15 June 1992

2

THE MYSTERY OF GOLF

It is generally agreed that golf has the finest literature of any game. It is also generally agreed that the principal reason for this is that golf is the only game played on natural terrain or on land shaped to resemble the terrain of the great Scottish linksland courses. It is the only outdoor game in which a player is faced with lifting a stationary ball from a stationary position.

Golf is a very exacting game. The golfer has to learn to play a wide assortment of shots. Through mistakes in judgment or execution, he frequently throws away the chance of posting the best score of his life on a course he admires enormously. The nature of golf changes with the wind and weather, and with the kind of competition the golfer is engaged in, be it singles at match play or medal play, foursomes or a four-ball game.

Many have tried to analyze why golf, despite the terrific punishment it inflicts on its faithful adherents, is such a fascinating game. Many have set down their opinions on this subject, but perhaps the man who has done it best is T. Arnold Hautain, a Canadian writer who flourished around the turn of the century. *The Mystery of Golf* was first published, in a limited edition of 440 copies, in 1908.

Early on Hautain comes to grips with his subject: he states that he believes there is no other game that makes as many demands as golf does on the man or woman whose aim is to play it consistently well. As he sees it, a golfer of the first class must not only possess exceptional physical coordination but a probing, attentive mind that works in happy coalescence with the movements of his body, the play of his emotions, and the steadfastness of his purpose. What is there in the game of golf which so differentiates it from all others that in it these trifling minutiae become magnified to matters of great moment as the mind plays a highly curious and important part?

Golf favours the player who combines strength with dexterity and, in this hard world with its ups and downs, what a priceless possession is golf with the endless beauty of its courses, the genial companionship of the clubhouse, and the game's inexhaustible lure!

It is said that you can detect national character in games. Golf is pre-eminently the game of the Scot: slow, sure, quiet, deliberate, canny even – each man playing for himself. There is no defensive play, no attacking an enemy's position, no subordination of oneself to the team, no coach to be obeyed, no relative positions of players. The weapon (club) is to the sportsman what the brush is to the artist or the pen to the poet. In golf there is never any reflex action possible. Every stroke must be played by the mind – gravely, quietly, deliberately. There is not a game known to sportsmen in which failure so exasperates.

Golf is the most jealous of mistresses. Are you worried and distrait; are you in debt and expecting a dun; are stocks unsteady and your margin small; is a note falling due; or has a more than ordinarily delicate feminine entanglement gone somewhat awry? Go not near the links. Take a country walk, or go for a ride; drop into the club and ask numerous friends to assuage their thirst; do anything rather than attempt the simple task of putting a little ball into a little hole. For to put that little ball into that little hole – or rather into those eighteen little holes – requires a mind absolutely unperturbed.

Golf is a game in which attitude of mind counts for incomparably more than mightiness of muscle. It is a physiological, psychological, and moral fight with yourself; it is a test of mastery over self; and the ultimate and irreducible element of the game is to determine which of the players is the more worthy combatant. Not only is golf an excellent test of character, it is also an excellent medicament for character. Moreover, it is a test of character in more ways than one: the cheat simply could not play golf – in the last resort no one would play with him.

Few things better reveal a man to himself than zealous and persistent efforts to decrease his handicap. Even it might be said that Tennyson's trinity of excellences – self-knowledge, self-reverence, self-control – are nowhere so worthily sought, or so efficacious when found, as on the links.

Golf requires the most concentrated mental attention. It requires also just as concentrated a moral attention. The moral factors are as important as the physical. He who succumbs to temptation will have to succumb to defeat!

Not only is the stroke in golf an extremely difficult one, it is also an extremely complicated one. No stroke in any other game is quite like it; so that proficiency in other games is neither a criterion of, nor a preparation for, proficiency in golf. Golf above all things needs the steadiest of nerves, the clearest eye, and the most imperturbable of brains. No kind of sport sooner finds out a man's weak point than does golf. Golf demands the training of a lifetime.

Yet not a little has been said, in a semi-sarcastic way, by devotees of other games than golf, about the comparative ease with which – as the sayers aver – a stationary ball can be struck as compared to one in motion. Those detractors forget the nicety of the stroke that is required. A tennis player has a whole court into which to play; a cricketer a whole field; the golfer has to put his ball into a hole the size of a jam pot, a quarter of a mile away! Indeed, the difficulties of golf are innumerable and incalculable.

Until a man has learned to keep his eye on the ball, he will not play golf, and not every good man will be a golfer; but I challenge anyone to dispute the fact that every really good golfer will at heart be a good man. Golf, in short, is not so much a game as it is a creed and a religion.

What is it that enables one man always to go round under eighty and another never? Whatever in its ultimate analysis mimicry may be – which is at the bottom of all education – the youthful caddie probably picks up the game by sheer unconscious imitation and the correct golfing swing comes to him with ease. If the physiologists are not all wrong, to excel in golf requires first of all a good brain, a good straight body, a good medulla and a good spinal cord to boot. All the nerve-cells and fibres must be educated, by constant practice, to perform smoothly, quickly, and forcibly the complex motions necessary for the peculiar stroke of golf.

Of a soul! If the physical mysteries of golf are so recondite, what of the psychic? In golf we see in its profoundest aspect that profound problem of the relation of mind to matter. Nowhere in the sum-total of the activities of life is this puzzle presented to us in a more acute shape than on the links. The links prove the fatal and irrefragable chain of cause and effect. Every golfer wills to excel, and every golfer sedulously searches for the causes of failure. Indeed, a veritable demon seems to enter into a man on the links. Few things bring home to us better the depths of our ignorance of ourselves than the mind's vagaries and eccentricities on the links.

It takes a great national cataclysm to throw up a great leader of men. Perhaps this is why an extraordinary round can be performed only by an extraordinary player.

What exasperates the ordinary man about golf is that it seems to be a game utterly and absolutely unamenable to reason – and this in spite of the fact that, on the links, it is on your own individual efforts that you count.

That golf is a game unique, need be proved to no golfer. He knows it only too well – often to his cost.

Is this uniqueness explicable? Well, perhaps in no other game, for one thing, are you obliged, or have you time, so intensely to concentrate your every faculty on your every stroke. In no other game have you so to be master of yourself, as it were, to steady yourself, your muscles, your nerves, your brain, nay, your mood, and your temper – or to be master of yourself for such a long stretch. One has to pass through much tribulation ere that feat is even approximately achieved. In no other game are you left so desperately alone. In no other game does all depend upon your individual effort. There is nothing to hamper you, nothing to hinder you, nothing to hurry you.

How golf betrays the character! You may have known a man for years, yet discover new traits in him on the links. Characteristics long buried beneath convention are suddenly resuscitated; foibles sedulously suppressed spring into existence; hereditary instincts lying dormant reveal themselves. Golf brings out idiosyncrasies and peculiarities. Sometimes it brings out more than these! The inexorability of the game is appalling, and may well unnerve the timorous player. Nothing in the rules of life and conduct is quite so rigid as are the conditions of this simple-seeming so-called game.

Golf is unique too in that it can be played anywhere – on lone seashores or crowded heaths, over high-road and hedge, amid moss and weed, on the veldt, on the prairie, on the meadow.

For high spirits and supple joints golf is too sedate. Enthusiasts will play world without end, as they have played it from time immemorial. Some two thousand years hence some golfers may have the temerity to affirm that golf is learned by playing golf, and not by some more rigid and scientific analysis of stroke. There is a fatefulness about golf that is terrorizing.

Among the psychological aspects of golf is its effect upon the character, and this is neither small nor unimportant. Whom golf loveth it chasteneth; and few men but come off the course chastened, and by consequence strengthened.

Golf is as serious as life. It admits no peccadillos; it permits no compromises; it recognizes no venial sins.

But the ultimate analysis of the mystery of golf is hopeless – as hopeless as the ultimate analysis of that of metaphysics or of that of the feminine heart. Fortunately, the hopelessness as little troubles the golfer as it does the philosopher or the lover!

Afterword

According to Editor Jerry Tarde's *Golf Digest* article of May 1993, in more modern times there has been a conspiracy to eliminate luck, specifically bad luck, from our wonderful game, when luck may be the only thing that keeps golf from turning into chess!

For example, the Rules of Golf have bowed to the conspiracy. The *stymie* was rendered extinct in 1951. There also used to be clubs called the *track iron* and *rut iron*, designed ingeniously to extricate the ball from unplayable lies; now if the ground is merely discoloured, you call over a rules official and get a *free drop,* modern golf's equivalent of welfare. As recently as 1959 you weren't allowed to lift and clean your ball on the putting green; now if there is even a forecast for cloudy skies, touring pros lift, clean and place their ball on the *fairway!*

In addition, in Hautain's day bunkers were *never* raked. Bunkers were never supposed to be places of pleasure, but cause for repentance. Today bunkers are raked to perfection, square-grooved clubs and short games are so precise it seems to be virtually impossible to take more than two strokes to get up and down from sixty or so yards away.

Similarly, golfers are now provided yardage books, flagstick-placement sheets and colour-coded flags to aim at. Not only have blind holes disappeared, being able to see the bottom of the flagstick from the tee is a must on most holes. Fairways and greens are over-watered to eliminate the bounce, particularly the bad bounce. As a consequence, very predictable target golf has replaced the more skilled pitch-and-run-up game.

In the constant striving for perfection and uniformity and – that most insidious goal of all – fairness, are we not losing what is at the heart of golf? Call it luck, or *rub of the green,* or unpredictability. But golf is a duller game without it.

Michael Bonallack, Secretary of the Royal and Ancient Golf Club of St. Andrews has noted that: "Bad luck should be a test of character. The champion learns to suck it up and get on with it. He knows that breaks even out over time, and he knows that the rest of us don't know this."

Luck is another name for variety, and judgment of that variety is an integral part of the game. *If we made people think more, there would not be such an emphasis on length as there is today.*

So, take heed those among us who would prefer to play ball-busting, straight-away 450-plus yard par fours; rather than be challenged by an ingenuous, thought-provoking lay-up or dog-leg hole.

In sum, we have spent enormous amounts of time, money, brain and computer power perfecting the design of golf courses, clubs and balls in a desperate effort to eliminate what all true golfers euphemistically refer to as the rub of the green. And yet, never have we ever come close to solving *the mystery of golf,* now 85 years since T. Arnold Hautain first published his famed treatise. Enough said.

21 May 1993

The Development of the Golf Ball, an historic record of its evolution, was commissioned by Hurley Style Limited of Hurley, Berkshire, England, and verified by the eminent golf historian and author David Stirk. The sub-plaques read, from left to right: wooden, circa 1590; feathery, circa 1790; gutta percha, circa 1850; machine gutty, circa 1880; Haskell, circa 1900; modern.

Bobby Jones (1902–1971) was hailed as the greatest golfer in the world – amateur or professional – by the age of twenty-three. He won thirteen major championships between 1923 and 1930, when he won the impregnable quadrilateral Grand Slam, and soon after retired from competitive golf at the age of twenty-eight. This 16-inch, limited-edition bronze (48/250) was sculpted by Karl Farris of Rancho Mirage, California, in 1991.

A circa 1930 Royal Doulton plate (D3395), measuring 10.5 inches and inscribed appropriately, *He Hath a Good Judgment Who Relieth Not Wholly On His Own.*

The Blackheath Goffer, painted by Lemuel Francis Abbott (1760–1803) in 1790, depicts William Innes, the captain, in his presidential uniform. This photogravure print was published in Edinburgh, circa 1901, and measures 25.75 x 18.5 inches

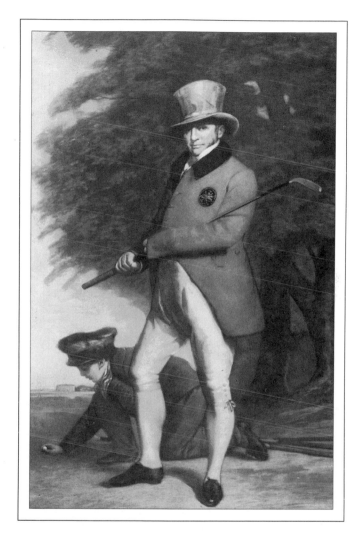

Painted by Sir John Watson Gordon (1788–1864), this portrait depicts *John Taylor,* a four-term captain of the Honourable Company of Edinburgh Golfers between 1807 and 1825. Engraved by Will Henderson and signed by him in pencil, this mezzotint was published in Britain by Vicar Brothers, circa 1914, and measures 19.75 x 13.0 inches.

The Tee, by Billy J. McCarroll of Lethbridge, Alberta. This 1990 artist's proof measures 18.75 x 9.5 inches.

Edmond G. Eberts and fellow member Robert B. Peterson at Beacon Hall Golf Club, Aurora, Ontario, May 1992, dressed by the The T. Barry Knicker Co. of Palm Desert, California.

Bruno, by Mary Anne Winterer of Montreal, Quebec. This 1986 artist's proof measures 20.5 x 11.5 inches. A plaque on the frame reads:

After 50 years of trying,
Ed Eberts finally scored his
first hole-in-one during the
75th Anniversary celebration at
Mount Bruno Country Club
June 26, 1993

3

GOLF-COURSE ARCHITECTURE

Introduction

Nineteen ninety-four marks the tenth anniversary of *The Turnberry Tour.* Along the way our honourable members will have had the opportunity to play eighty-eight wonderful golf courses in England, Scotland, Ireland and Northern Ireland, the United States of America and Canada, twenty of which were ranked in 1993 by *Golf Magazine* as being among the *100 greatest courses in the world/United States.*

As I've had the privilege to play twenty-six of the ultimate 100 courses in the world, thirty-three of North America's best, and countless other wonderful challenges over the past fifty years, I thought it appropriate to make a comment about golf-course architecture. And while I do not claim to be a so-called *expert,* I will admit to appreciating the talents of the great masters, some of whom have written books for true golfers to enjoy.

Books on Golf-Course Architecture

The first book about the best courses in Great Britain dates back to 1891, written by Horace Hutchinson, the winner of the British Amateur Championship in 1886 and 1887. It was called *Famous Golf Links.* In 1910 Bernard Darwin produced his milestone book, *The Golf Courses of the British Isles.*

The first books on golf-course architecture written by golf-course architects appeared in the 1920s when golf enjoyed a tremendous boom following the end of the first World War. During that decade, no fewer than seven books on the subject appeared.

The first of these, a small but substantial book by Dr. Alister Mackenzie called *Golf Architecture,* was published in London in 1920, as was *Some Essays in Golf-Course Architecture* by Harry S. Colt and C. Hugh Alison. *The Links,* by Wiles Robert Hunter, came out in 1926. The following year saw publication of *Golf Architecture in America: Its Strategy and Construction* by George C. Thomas, Jr.

In 1928 another important book largely about golf-course architecture appeared: Charles Blair Macdonald's *Scotland's Gift – Golf.* Macdonald was a founding member of the USGA in 1894, and won the first US Amateur Championship at the Newport Country Club in Rhode Island in 1895. *The Architectural Side of Golf,* published in London in 1929, was written by two Englishmen, H. N. Wethered and Thomas Simpson. Wethered also brought out *The Perfect Golfer,* a series of extended essays, in 1931.

Six Great Masters of Golf-Course Architecture

The (-/-) denotes the 1993 biennial rankings by *Golf Magazine* of the 100 greatest courses in the world/United States.

Before discussing thoughts to do with golf-course architecture let us recognize the incredible contribution of six great masters whose magnificent legacy spans the period 1864 to 1936, namely: Old Tom Morris (3/-), Donald Ross (7/11), Dr. Alister Mackenzie (10/6), the partnership of Harry S. Colt and C. Hugh Alison (10/2), and Albert W. Tillinghast (7/9), who combined are credited with designing or redesigning thirty-seven of the *Golf Magazine* ranked 100 greatest courses in the world and a total of twenty-six of the best 100 in the United States. For further information please refer to Appendix 1, page 37.

In examining the 1993 list in greater detail, it is interesting to note that an additional ten British and nineteen American courses, built before 1935, are also included in the *Golf Magazine* 100 greatest courses in the world/United States ranking. In sum, sixty-six of the 100 best courses in the world today were originally designed and built more than fifty years ago. And, despite the fact that many thousands of additional golf courses have subsequently been built worldwide, what is it about the aforementioned classics that makes them so special? Read on!

The Dr. Alister Mackenzie Legacy

By the turn of this century golfers recognized that golf was both most appealing and rewarding when it was played on courses laid out on gently rolling land, like the linksland along the sea in St. Andrews. There was also general agreement that more appealing holes could be fashioned on inland courses by moving earth here and there to create more suitable sites for tees, more interesting routes from tee to green, more intriguing hazards, more receptive greens and a number of good pin positions. There was an art to it all and golf holes of *strategic design* not only encouraged bold play but they also punished the golfer who accepted the challenge that a certain hole presented but failed to produce the required shots.

The leaders in golf-course architecture clearly realized early on that an alternative route from tee to green should be presented on a long par-4 and every par-5 hole. And, while golf-course architecture was a glamorous, self-fulfilling profession, it was also a difficult one. Its ideal practitioner needed to have the soul of an artist, the brain of an engineer, and the heart of a golfer.

For many, Dr. Alister Mackenzie's *Golf Architecture* is the most informative and interesting of the early books on golf-course architecture written by a member of that profession, published in 1920 when the author was fifty years of age. Though not a charming literary adventure, it is primarily the work of a man trying to get down on paper his ideas, some obvious and others recondite, about the multiple considerations that go into designing and maintaining a sound, stimulating course that both the professional and the average golfer will *enjoy* rather than be intimidated by while playing.

Mackenzie enumerated the thirteen *essential features* of an ideal golf course, but he also wished to emphasize some fundamental points such as these:

- *The chief objective of every golf architect or greenkeeper worth his salt is to imitate the beauties of nature so closely as to make his work indistinguishable from nature itself.*

- *Most golfers have an entirely erroneous view of the real objective of hazards. The majority of them simply look upon hazards as a means of punishing a bad shot, when their real objective is to make the game interesting.*

- *Hazards should be placed with an objective and none should be made which has not some influence on the line of play to the hole.*

- *On many courses there are far too many bunkers: the sides of the fairways are riddled with them, and many of these courses would be equally interesting if half of the bunkers were turfed over as grassy hollows.*

- *On a seaside course in particular little construction work is necessary; the most important thing is to make the fullest possible use of existing features.*

His goal of striving to create testing but natural-looking holes could not be more different than that of all too many modern golf-course architects who are adding to the plethora of strange new courses now finding a place on the PGA Tour.

A hole of strategic design asks the golfer to make his/her way from tee to green by playing to the left or right of a hazard unless s/he is able to carry it. Mackenzie clearly spells out his main points.

The differences that make a hole really interesting are usually those in which a great advantage can be gained in successfully accomplishing heroic carries over hazards of an impressive appearance, or in taking great risks in placing a shot so as to gain a big advantage for the next. Holes of this description not only cater for great judgment, but great skill: a man or woman who has such confidence that s/he can place his/her ball within a few feet of the objective gains a big advantage over the opponent who dares not to take similar risks. An ideal golf hole should provide an infinite variety of shots according to the various positions of the tee, the situation of the flagstick, the direction and strength of the wind, etc.

I believe that the real reason St. Andrews Old Course is infinitely superior to anything else is owing to the fact that it was constructed when no one knew anything about the subject at all, and since it has been considered too sacred to be touched. And so, economy in course construction consists in obtaining the best possible results at a minimum of cost. The more one sees of golf courses, the more one realizes the importance of doing construction really well, so that it is likely to be of a permanent character. It is impossible to lay too much emphasis on the importance of finality.

Following on, it is interesting to consider Mackenzie's thirteen essential features of an ideal golf course.

   1. The course, where possible, should be arranged in two loops of nine holes.

2. *There should be a large proportion of good two-shot holes, two or three drive-and-pitch holes, and at least four one-shot holes.*

3. *There should be little walking between the greens and tees, and the course should be arranged so that in the first instance there is always a slight walk forwards from the green to the next tee; then the holes are sufficiently elastic to be lengthened in the future if necessary.*

4. *The greens and fairways should be sufficiently undulating, but there should be no hill climbing.*

5. *Every hole should have a different character.*

6. *There should be a minimum of blindness for the approach shots.*

7. *The course should have beautiful surroundings, and all the artificial features should have so natural an appearance that a stranger is unable to distinguish them from nature itself.*

8. *There should be sufficient number of heroic carries from the tee, but the course should be arranged so that the weaker player with the loss of a stroke or portion of a stroke shall always have an alternative route open to him/her.*

9. *There should be an infinite variety in the strokes required to play the various holes – viz., interesting brassy shots, iron shots, pitch-and-run-up shots.*

10. *There should be a complete absence of the annoyance and irritation caused by the necessity of searching for lost balls.*

11. *The course should be so interesting that even the plus player is consistently stimulated to improve his/her game in attempting shots s/he has hitherto been unable to play.*

12. The course should be so arranged that the long handicap player, or even the absolute beginner, should be able to enjoy his/her round in spite of the fact that s/he is piling up a big score.

13. The course should be equally good during winter and summer, the texture of the greens and fairways should be perfect, and the approaches should have the same consistency as the greens.

Given Dr. Alister Mackenzie's aforementioned essential features, he further suggested that the most serious mistake made by a golf committee is believing in the fallacy they will save money by neglecting to obtain the services of an accomplished architect for the course, or for any new work on the course, and focusing instead on the clubhouse, as inevitably many more costly errors are made in constructing the former than in building the latter.

The expert in golf architecture has to be intimately conversant with the theory of playing the game but this has no connection with the physical skill in playing it. An ideal golf-course expert should also have what might be termed an artistic temperament and vivid imagination, and the training should be mental, not physical.

Finally, *it may at first appear unreasonable that the question of aesthetics should enter into golf-course design; however, on deeper analysis, it becomes clear that the great courses, and in detail all the famous holes and greens, are fascinating to the golfer by reason of their shape, their situation, and the character of their modelling. When these elements obey the fundamental laws of balance, of harmony, and fine proportion they give rise to what we call beauty. This excellence of design is more felt than fully realized by the player, but nevertheless it is constantly exercising a subconscious influence upon him/her, and in course of time s/he grows to admire such a course as all works of beauty are eventually felt and admired.*

Afterword

In sum, the great master golf-course architects understood that there was an art to it all. They readily appreciated the significance of strategic design. Their greatest courses were very well constructed, respecting the importance of finality. Attendant greenkeepers nurtured the terrain and naturalized the surroundings. Championships were held to challenge the par and generations of custodians continued to cherish the sanctity of these wonderful legacies. So too should we!

7 January 1994

4

How to Improve the Pace of Play
Answers to Golf's Greatest Dilemma

Introduction

Though its origins have been traced back to the Middle Ages, golf remains a humbling game at the best of times!

Generally regarded as the oldest golf club in the world, The Gentleman Golfers of Leith, Scotland, later to be called the Honourable Company of Edinburgh Golfers, was founded in 1744. Today it is more commonly referred to as Muirfield.

The Royal and Ancient Golf Club of St. Andrews, though founded ten years later in 1754, was to become known as the home of golf. Together, the R&A and the United States Golf Association (USGA) set policy with regard to the Rules of Golf.

The founding of the Montreal Golf Club in 1873 marked the organization of the very first golf club in North America, bestowed the *Royal* title by Queen Victoria in 1884. The first permanent club in the United States, the St. Andrew's Golf Club in Yonkers, New York, was founded four years later in 1877.

According to the National Golf Foundation in Jupiter, Florida, 21.7 million Americans played golf at least once in 1988. How many golfers, as opposed to duffers, that figure represents is another question! A very vague rule of thumb in golf today suggests that twenty-five percent of the people who play record seventy-five percent of the rounds.

As of 1988 there were 2.2 million playing golf in Canada and the number has been rising by twelve percent per year since 1984. Each of our country's then 1,797 regulation courses, double the 825 courses that existed in 1972, averaged 35,000 rounds annually.

Slow play has been described as a curse in golf, a continent-wide epidemic afflicting professional tour players, weekend duffers and everyone in between. The *pace of play*, as it is euphemistically referred to, is a thorny problem for those involved in the most honourable of athletic pursuits. It is oft said, *A slow player can slow down a fast player, but a fast player can't speed up a slow player.*

We beg to differ. Read on, take note and enjoy!

The USGA Guidelines

The United States Golf Association has tried to take a firm stance on the issue in the conduct of its championships. But if anything, the US Open, played on the most difficult courses set up to provide the ultimate challenge, bordered by punishing rough, only magnifies the problem. Furthermore, USGA attempts to enforce Rule 6-7, *the player shall play without undue delay*, have met with mixed results at best.

Even so, a two-page memo outlining the USGA guidelines states that in the first two rounds of the US Open, when competitors play three-ball games, they are expected to take no more than thirteen-and-a-half minutes per hole, four hours and three minutes for the round. After the cut, when two-ball games are played, times are adjusted to twelve minutes a hole and three hours and thirty-six minutes for the round. Obviously, two-ball games play much faster than three- and four-ball games.

In my experience, having challenged more than 300 different courses over the past forty-five years, club players and their guests should easily match and even better the USGA guidelines. The courses we play are never set up to US Open standards, seldom bordered by six to twelve-inch rough. Neither are the pressures of competition as great; nor the spectators, photographers and TV cameramen as trying. Take heed.

Playing with Your Spouse

Playing with your spouse on the golf course runs almost as great a marital risk as getting caught with someone else's anywhere else! Worse still, more often than not, mixed four-ball games tend to take longer to play a round than any other combination of golfers.

Try to treat your husband or wife exactly as you would your regular golfing partner. Don't offer advice or make comments when you would not do the same to your regular partner. The *not-so-friendly discussion* that will inevitably follow such advice takes up valuable playing time. Too much supervision only stifles instinct. The fact is you are not a golf professional. What makes you think you can teach your spouse, just because you're married to her/him?

The most important thing in mixed golf is to throw away all emotion when you play with your wife/husband. Don't get any more emotionally involved than you would with your best friend. Just as you should not bring the office home with you at night, you shouldn't bring the strains of domestic strife with you to the golf course!

Rather, it's the spirit of the game that counts. So keep your head steady, take a full shoulder turn on your backswing and follow through to your target. Keep your thoughts to yourself and, most importantly, maintain the pace of play!

Golf Etiquette

If the guidelines set out by the USGA are to be adhered to, you must always allow faster players to play through. Without question, three- and four-ball games must wave two-ball games to play through. Similarly, players failing to maintain the pace of play by looking for a ball or by dropping back more than one clear hole from those in front, *must* immediately wave the following group to play through.

If the group playing in front of yours has allowed a clear hole in front of them, *it is your right and responsibility to request to play through.* It is also your responsibility *to remain clear of the group following yours.* If you find your group holding up the next group, you must wave them through, even if the real culprits are the group playing ahead of yours, as you have failed to honour your responsibility and right to play through. As such, you may never claim that the pace of play is someone else's fault. It's yours for now and evermore, nobody else's.

Power Cart Tips

If you are going to carry your clubs, be prepared to maintain 3.0 mph on the inclines and a 3.5 mph pace on level ground. Power carts operate best full speed ahead. Needless to say, you must obey all cart direction signs and keep the carts on the pathways where provided; they're there for a very good reason!

As you will most likely be sharing a cart, you need not drive up to every shot. Rather, leave the cart for the furthest-to-the-flagstick player and walk ahead to your own ball, club or clubs in hand prepared to play when it's your turn. If there is a bunker between you and the green, don't forget to also take along your sand wedge and always bring your putter. As such you are prepared to play the next shot(s) as required and without further delay.

Park the cart to the side of the green closest to the next tee. In so doing you will not have to walk back to retrieve it after you've putted out. The same holds true for golfers who prefer to carry.

Always Be Ready to Play Your Next Shot

The honour system is said to be an obstacle to fast, efficient play. Wrong! It's not the system – it may well be the honouree! Even so, whether or not you have the honour, always be prepared and ready to play your next shot. You must play a provisional ball if there's any question as to the whereabouts of your previous shot. By so doing you will regain your composure, never to impede the pace of play.

As you approach to play a fairway shot, you should have predetermined the distance to the middle of the green; whether the flagstick is located at the front, middle or back of the green; the position of the green-side bunkers; the direction and relative velocity of the wind; and, have selected the club you will play once it's your turn.

Upon reaching the green, repair your ballmark carefully, mark and clean your ball. Allow the furthest-from-the-hole player to putt first. When it's your turn, you should be ready to putt without delay. As such, take care to read the green in advance and putt continuously providing you are not interfering with an opponent's line of play.

Once you've putted out, head directly to the next hole. Scores should only be recorded on reaching the next tee.

How Not to Lose Golf Clubs

One wonders how so many golf clubs go missing during the course of play. Notwithstanding, we do know that better than ninety percent of the time clubs are *lost* in the rough within six feet of the fairways, the bunkers and greens! What to do?

If you have two or more clubs in hand and have decided which to play next, the extra club(s) should be placed within sight on the fairway or green, never dropped out-of-sight, out-of-mind in the rough. Furthermore, upon reaching the putting surface, your extra clubs should forthwith be placed on the green, near the apron, in line with the pathway to the next tee. As such, your clubs will never go missing, you will never have to retrace your steps to retrieve them and, most importantly, you will never impede the pace of play!

It's also a good idea to have your clubs name tagged. Should you find someone else's club on/off the course, please hand it in to the proshop at the very first opportunity.

Ballmarks, Bunkers, Divots and Debris

Nothing is more annoying than a beautiful green scarred by ballmarks; a poorly raked bunker and finding your ball in a footprint; a lush green fairway littered with loose divots and debris scattered about the course by uncaring golfers.

The best way to fix a ballmark is to insert the repair fork just outside the back of the divot hole. Pull the back of the divot towards the centre of the pit mark, not up. Pull both sides of the ballmark into the centre. This should close the hole. Then gently tap the ballmark level with your putter. Please refer to Appendix 2 on page 39 for a more graphic explanation.

While you are at it, fix another ballmark or two. Your leadership will be much appreciated by the greenkeeper, and help to maintain the pace of play.

A poorly raked bunker not only upsets the player, it will inevitably upset the pace of play. So please take care to rake the bunker properly after you've played your shot. Taking two hands to achieve an even surface takes less time than attempting a mediocre one-handed effort.

Divots too need be replaced with care. Many a properly replaced divot will grow anew. In any event, by repairing a divot you are protecting the roots of the displaced grass, and nature will see to it that the fairway or rough will grow back with time. Furthermore, be careful not to take a divot with a practice swing – better golfers and professionals never do!

Debris is an insult to all who profess to be golfers. Please do your part to contain the debris and clean up for others as you must.

Please always pick up your tees, broken or otherwise, and never pound one into the ground in disgust. If you don't do your part, the maintenance staff will have to before the next mowing. As a point of interest, US golfers mash, mangle and generally dispatch more than one billion tees annually!

The Ultimate Cost of Slow Play

Assuming that a four-ball game may book to tee off every eight minutes, 7.5 x 4 = 30 golfers per hour, and if the course is unnecessarily tied up due to slow play for an extra hour every morning and afternoon, the ultimate cost is: eighteen lost green fees (assuming a thirty percent guest factor) and fifteen lost power cart charges (assuming fifty percent utilization) per day. With green fees at $50 and a cart charge of $22, the unrealized revenue per day is $1,230; $8,610 per week; $36,900 per month; $221,400 per season. The per season figure is the equivalent of one-third of what it costs per annum to maintain a *championship* golf course.

Yes – slow play is very expensive, as inevitably the members must cover any shortfall in revenue. So every time you fail to maintain the USGA guideline pace of play – think about the money it's costing you personally. Respect your course marshalls as they are doing their damndest to earn their keep! Finally, by seeing to it that the proper pace of play is maintained, your concentration will improve. Your swing will be more relaxed and consistently better shots will be played with the result that you will record lower scores, as will be the case for all golfers, at every level of proficiency. Could you ask for anything more!

Afterword

Golf is a wonderful game, to be enjoyed by those who appreciate and respect the privilege of playing a well-maintained course in a magnificent setting, every hole a painting to behold and a challenge to play.

Slow play must never be tolerated. The pace of play must be the concern of every professional, weekend duffer and dedicated golfer alike. Remember too, *fast play makes for fast friends.*

As to the care of the course, *The Proof of the Golfer* by Edgar A. Guest (1881–1959) perhaps says it best. Refer to Appendix 3, page 40.

11 September 1989

APPENDIX 1

The Legacy of Six Great Architects

The (-/-) denotes the 1993 biennial rankings by *Golf Magazine* of the 100 greatest courses in the world/United States:

Old Tom Morris, the custodian of the Old Course at *St. Andrews* (8/-), designed *Royal Dornoch* (13/-) in 1886, *Royal County Down* (7/-) in 1889 and *Lahinch* (89/-) in 1893.

Donald Ross who grew up playing *Royal Dornoch* is remembered by his work at *Pinehurst* (No.2) (11/7) in 1903, *Scioto* (52/33) in 1912, *Wannamoisett* (-/65) in 1916, *Oakland Hills* (South) (22/13) in 1917, *Inverness* (51/32) and the redesign of *Interlachen* (-/85) in 1919, *Plainfield* (97/60) in 1920, *Oakland Hills* (East) (37/21) with Robert T. Jones, Jr. and *Salem* (-/80) in 1926, *Aronimink* (-/100) in 1928 and *Seminole* (19/11) in 1929.

Dr. Alister Mackenzie designed *Kingstone Heath* (35/-) and redesigned *Royal St. George's* (Sandwich) (26/-) in 1925. In 1926 he built *Royal Melbourne* (5/-), *Royal Adelaide* (53/-), *New South Wales* (59/-) and the *Valley Club of Montecito* (-/64). The *Victoria* (71/-) course followed in 1927. *Cypress Point* (2/2) dates to 1928 and *Pasatiempo* (100/61) to 1929. *Augusta National* (4/4) with Robert T. Jones, Jr. and *Crystal Downs* (15/9) were built in 1932. The *Ohio State* (Scarlet Course) (-/94) with Perry Maxwell was laid out in 1934.

The partnership of Harry S. Colt and C. Hugh Alison was in a class by itself, though the partners generally worked on individual projects.

Colt designed *Ganton* (68/-) in 1891. He assisted George Crump in the development of *Pine Valley* (1/1) in 1918. In 1920 he was involved in the redesign of *Sunningdale* (Old Course) (39/-) and in laying out *Royal Portrush* (18/-) in Northern Ireland. In 1924 he designed *Wentworth* (61/-) with John Stanton Fleming Morrison. He was entrusted with the revision of *Royal Liverpool* (Hoylake) (78/-) in 1925 and *Muirfield* (6/-) in 1926.

Alison designed the *Country Club of Detroit* (-/86) in 1914. He was responsible for the first modern courses in Japan. With Kinya Fujita, the designer of *Kasumigaseki* (East) (54/-), he worked to improve the enchanting course in 1929. He designed *Hirono* (40/-) near Kobe in 1932 and co-designed *Kawana* (50/-) in 1936 with Kinya Fujita.

Albert W. Tillinghast is credited with the design of classics the likes of *San Francisco* (33/18) in 1915, *Somerset Hills* (84/52) in 1918, *Baltusrol* (Lower) (30/16) with Robert T. Jones, Jr. in 1922, *Wingfoot* (West) (17/10) and (East) (83/51) in 1923, *Quaker Ridge* (41/23) and *Baltimore* (Five Farms East) (95/58) in 1926, *Ridgewood* (West/East) (-/79) in 1929 and *Bethpage* (Black) (-/92) in 1936.

GREAT SHOT!

But you left a ballmark.

Do you know what to do?

Only you can prevent ballmark damage!

WRONG!

Pulling on the centre or the sides will leave the centre raised – to be scalped by the next mower!

RIGHT (1)

Insert green repair tool just outside the back of the divot hole. Pull the back of the divot towards the centre of the pit mark (not up).

RIGHT (2)

Pull both sides of ball mark into the centre. This should close the hole. Then gently tap the ball-mark down with your putter.

Remember:

WRONG!

Do not pull up with green repair tool. This will only bring sand to the surface.

RIGHT

Insert tool and pull forward.

APPENDIX 3

The Proof of a Golfer
by Edgar A. Guest

The proof of the pudding is in the eating they say,
But the proof of a golfer is not
The number of strokes he takes in a day
Or the skill he puts into a shot.
There's more to the game than the score which you make;
Here's a truth which all golfers endorse:
You don't prove your worth by the shots which you make,
But the care which you take of the course.

A golfer is more than a ball-driving brute;
He is more than a mug-hunting czar.
To be known as a golfer, you don't have to shoot
The course of your home club in par.
But you do have to love every blade of grass,
Every inch of the fairway and greens.
If you don't take care of the course as you pass,
You're not what a *good golfer* means.

Just watch a good golfer some day when you're out,
And note what he does when he plays.
He never goes on leaving divots about;
'Til the grass is put back in, that's where he stays.
Observe him in bunkers as he stands for his shot.
Then note when the ball has been played,
He never unthinkingly turns from the spot
'Til he's covered the footprints he made.

You may brag of your scores and may boast of your skill.
You may think as a golfer you're good;
But if footprints you make, in traps you don't fill,
You don't love the game as you should.
For your attitude unto the sport you enjoy
Isn't proven by brilliance or force.
The proof of the golfer – now get this my boy –
Is the care that you take of the course.

REFERENCES

THE ROYAL AND ANCIENT GAME OF GOLF

Browning, Robert. *A History of Golf.* London: J.M. Dent and Sons Ltd., 1955.*

Macdonald, Charles Blair. *Scotland's Gift – Golf.* New York and London: Charles Scribner's Sons, 1928.*

THE MYSTERY OF GOLF

Hautain, T. Arnold. *The Mystery of Golf.* Boston and New York: Houghton Mifflin Company, 1908.*

GOLF-COURSE ARCHITECTURE

Mackenzie, Alister. *Golf Architecture.* London: Simpkin, Marshall, Hamilton, Kent & Co., 1920.*

"The 1993 biennial rankings of the 100 Greatest Courses in the world/United States," *Golf Magazine*, November 1993.

HOW TO IMPROVE THE PACE OF PLAY

Platts, Michael. *Illustrated History of Golf.* London: Bison Books Ltd., 1988.

"Canada: The Par North," *Town & Country*, June 1988.

"Club Corp. Makes Clubs Pay," *Fortune*, November 12, 1984.

"Playing With Your Spouse," *Golf Digest*, May 1987.

"Identifying the slow-play culprits on tour," *Golf Digest*, July 1989.

" The Boom in Golf as Baby Boomers Hit The Links," *Business Week*, March 27, 1989.

"The Explosive Future of Golf," *Golf Digest*, March 1989.

* Available through Robert Macdonald, publisher of The Classics of Golf, 65 Commerce Road, Stamford, CT 06902, USA.

Edmond G. Eberts

Born in Montreal, Quebec, Canada, in 1938, Ed Eberts was introduced to the mystery of golf at the tender age of five. Early on he was a Class A caddie and an active junior golfer. More recently he has been involved in the formation of several private golf clubs and acts as the Membership Committee Chairman for The Turnberry Tour, an international invitational golf classic.

He is a member of the Royal and Ancient Golf Club of St. Andrews, Scotland, and PGA West in La Quinta, California, USA. In Canada he plays at Mount Bruno Country Club near Montreal, Quebec, and The Glencoe Golf and Country Club in Calgary, Alberta, enjoying Round Table privileges at Redtail Golf Club near London, Ontario. At Beacon Hall Golf Club in Aurora, Ontario, he was honoured to serve as a Director, Chairman of the Golf Committee and the first ever Captain, responsible for drafting the rules, the regulations and the competition schedules – and for dramatically improving the pace of play!

Ed Eberts has an extensive library of golf literature and an eclectic collection of historic and contemporary golf art.